)

DATE DUE

The Library of
NATIVE AMERICANS

The Adena, Hopewell, and Fort Ancient

of Ohio

Greg Roza

The Rosen Publishing Group's
PowerKids Press™
New York

For Dad and Kathy

Special thanks to Jack Blosser

Published in 2005 by The Rosen Publishing Group, Inc.
29 East 21st Street, New York, NY 10010

Photo and Illustration Credits: Cover © The Field Museum, A110028c, Photographer Ron Testa; p. 4 Mindy Liu; p. 6 © Tim Thompson/Corbis; p. 9 Library of Congress, Geography and Map Division; pp. 10, 33, 36 © Werner Forman/Art Resource, NY; p. 13 Still Picture Branch, National Archives and Records Administration (ARC 558105); pp. 14, 19, 22, 27, 40 Ohio Historical Society; pp. 17, 28, 31, 47, 54–55 © North Wind Picture Archives; p. 21 Rosen Publishing Group; p. 24 © Louis Glanzman; Courtesy National Park Service; p. 35 © The Field Museum, A86135; p. 38 Andrew Sawyer/SunWatch Indian Village/Archaeological Park; p. 42 © Richard A. Cooke/Corbis; pp. 44, 53 © Corbis; p. 51 © David Muench/CORBIS

Book Design: Erica Clendening
Book Layout, Adena, Hopewell, and Fort Ancient Art, and Production: Mindy Liu
Contributing Editor: Shira Laskin

Library of Congress Cataloging-in-Publication Data

Roza, Greg.
    The Adena, Hopewell, and Fort Ancient of Ohio / Greg Roza.— 1st ed.
    p. cm. — (The library of Native Americans)
    Includes index.
    ISBN 1-4042-2874-8 (lib. bdg.)
    1. Adena culture. 2. Hopewell culture. 3. Fort Ancient culture. 4. Mounds—Ohio. 5.
    Ohio—Antiquities. I. Title. II. Series.

    E99.A18R69 2005
    977.1'01—dc22
                                                    2004002091

Manufactured in the United States of America

There are a variety of terminologies that have been employed when writing about Native Americans. There are sometimes differences between the original language used by a Native American group for certain names or vocabulary and the anglicized or modernized versions of such names or terms. Although this book contains terms that we feel will be most recognizable to our readership, there may also exist synonymous or native words that are preferred by certain speakers.

Contents

Where the Adena, Hopewell, and Fort Ancient Lived

Illinois

Indiana

Ohio

West Virginia

Kentucky

Atlantic Ocean

Areas where the Adena, Hopewell, and Fort Ancient lived

Canada

United States

Atlantic Ocean

Gulf of Mexico

One

Introducing the Adena, Hopewell, and Fort Ancient Cultures

The Woodland Period refers to the years from 800 B.C. to 1200 A.D.—a time in which three select cultures of Native Americans lived in Ohio and the surrounding area. These cultures were the Adena, Hopewell, and Fort Ancient. Two of these three Native American cultures, the Adena and the Hopewell, are known as mound builders. The Adena and Hopewell cultures shared the tradition of building mounds and earthworks from around 1000–800 B.C. to around 400–500 A.D. Throughout the Early and Middle Woodland Periods, the Adena and Hopewell constructed mounds of earth. Many of these mounds were graves used for burying the dead. Other mounds and earthworks were built for different purposes. Although the people of the Fort Ancient culture are not recognized for their mound-building efforts, experts have identified a small number of mounds that were built by them.

The Woodland Period is part of what is known as prehistory. Prehistory, 13,000 B.C. to 1650 A.D., is the time before written records of history were kept in the Ohio area. No one knows the exact story of the people who lived during this time. There are no written accounts to provide this information. Scientists rely on artifacts and other evidence to figure out what life was like for these

This map shows the Ohio Region, the area in which the Adena, Hopewell, and Fort Ancient lived.

6 The Bering Land Bridge National Preserve is the remainder of the land bridge that many scientists believe connected Asia with North America more than 13,000 years ago. It is about 500 miles (804.7 km) northwest of Anchorage, Alaska.

ancient people. The information we have about the Woodland Period is based on scientific explorations of the mounds and village sites left by the Adena, Hopewell, and Fort Ancient peoples.

Cultures Before the Adena, Hopewell, and Fort Ancient

Most scholars believe that between 40,000 and 13,000 years ago, people traveled from Asia to North America by crossing a frozen land bridge that connected the continents. These were the first Americans. They spread out through the Americas, settling in different places. By about 12,000 years ago, some of these people had reached the southern tip of South America.

Evidence suggests that people have lived in the area in and around Ohio since 13,000 B.C. Scientists use four periods of time to discuss these people and their traditions. Since there are no written accounts from these times, the periods are based on scientific estimates of when cultural traditions changed. As a result of this estimation, the periods of time often overlap.

The first period is called the Paleo-Indian Period. This refers to the people who lived in the Ohio region between 13,000 B.C. and 8000 B.C. The second period is called the Archaic Period and includes the people who lived in the area between 8000 B.C. and 1000 B.C. The third period is the Woodland Period. It is broken into four parts: the Early Woodland Period, 1000 B.C.–100 B.C.; the Middle Woodland Period, 100 B.C.–400 A.D.; the Late Woodland Period, 500 A.D.–900 A.D.; and the Late Prehistoric Period, 900 A.D. to the time of European contact, around 1650–1700 A.D. The Early Woodland Period involved the Adena culture, the Middle Woodland involved the Hopewell culture, and the Late Prehistoric Period involved the Fort Ancient culture. The fourth period of time is known as the Historic Period. It refers to the time from when Europeans first came to North America.

Periods of History in the Ohio Region

Paleo-Indian Period	13,000 B.C. – 8000 B.C.
Archaic Period	8000 B.C. – 1000 B.C.
Woodland Period	1000 B.C. – 1650 A.D. to 1700 A.D.
Early Woodland Period	1000 B.C. – 100 B.C.
Middle Woodland Period	100 B.C. – 400 A.D.
Late Woodland Period	500 A.D. – 900 A.D.
Late Prehistoric Period	900 A.D. – 1650 A.D. to 1700 A.D.
Historic Period	1650 A.D. to 1700 A.D. – present

The Adena and Hopewell cultures lived near the Ohio River. This 1776 map shows the river's many tributaries, or smaller streams and rivers that lead into the Ohio River.

Early Mound Builders

The cultural tradition of burying people in mounds can be traced back to the Late Archaic Period in the northern half of Ohio. During this time, a burial ritual involving natural mounds, called glacial kames, was practiced by a group of people. A kame is a layered mound of sand and gravel left over after the melting of a glacier. At the end of the last ice age, a period of time when thick sheets of ice covered much of Earth, melting glaciers left kames across North America as they disappeared. These naturally existing mounds ranged from a few feet to 100 feet (30.5 m) high.

10 This decorative collar, featuring a carved animal, is believed to be an artifact from the time of the Glacial Kame culture. It is known as a gorget.

Early on, this group was named the Glacial Kame culture for their tradition of burying their dead in kames. Today, however, archaeologists realize that there is not enough evidence to separate these people as a different culture from the others who lived around them. As a result of this, the culture is now referred to as a Late Archaic group who practiced the ritual of burying their dead in glacial kames.

The mounds of this Late Archaic group often contained the remains of many people that were buried in a variety of ways. Most bodies were placed in a curled or sleeping position. Some bodies were buried lying down. Others were placed sitting up. Other methods involved a bundling of disassembled bones. The burial tradition also included placing different objects in the mounds with the dead. This included polished stones, pipes, and decorative collars worn around the neck, known as gorgets.

This Late Archaic group who practiced the ritual of burying their dead in glacial kames made use of *natural* mounds of earth, unlike the cultures of the Woodland Period. The fact that they buried so many of their dead within these mounds suggests that the group may have lived in other areas and made return visits to bury their dead at certain times of the year. Most scholars believe that this Late Archaic group moved less frequently than their ancestors had. However, they moved more frequently than the cultures of the Woodland Period.

Mounds of the Adena, Hopewell, and Fort Ancient

During the Early and Middle Woodland Periods, the Adena and Hopewell people continued and expanded the practice of burying their dead in mounds of earth. Each cultural group brought their own distinct customs, beliefs, and lifestyles into the tradition, including the creation of man-made mounds. The mounds created during the Early and Middle Woodland Periods are unique to the cultural group that lived during each time. Later, during the Late Prehistoric Period, the Fort Ancient culture continued this practice on a much smaller scale.

Some of these mounds still exist today. Archaeologists, or scientists who study the past by carefully excavating and examining artifacts and other features, have studied these mounds. By recognizing the differences between the mounds, such as shape and size, archaeologists have determined which mounds were built by the Adena, Hopewell, and Fort Ancient people.

The information we have about the Adena, Hopewell, and Fort Ancient is very limited when compared to the evidence we have about historic Native American groups. Although prehistoric evidence was left behind, much of it did not survive. Many objects were made of perishable materials, or things that would decay over time. Scientists have used the evidence that did survive to make educated guesses about how and when the Adena, Hopewell, and Fort Ancient existed. Their understanding of these cultures offers us a glimpse into the lives of the people who inhabited the Ohio Region so many years ago.

This 1977 photograph shows a scientist from the Cleveland Museum of Natural History. He is recording information as he stands on Gleeson Mound, a Hopewell burial mound near Cleveland, Ohio.

Two

The Adena

The beginning of the Woodland Period, from 1000 B.C. to around 100 B.C., is called the Early Woodland Period. During this time, the Adena people occupied the Ohio Region. The Adena culture flourished in southern Ohio and southern Indiana, to southeast Illinois. Their culture also spread from central Ohio down through the middle of Kentucky and into the middle of West Virginia. The name Adena comes from the name of the estate of Thomas Worthington, who was governor of Ohio during the early part of the 1800s. Adena Mound was discovered on his property.

Adena Life

The Native Americans who lived in the Ohio area in the years before the Woodland Period had different lifestyles from the Adena. The Native Americans of the Paleo-Indian Period were mostly nomads, or people who moved around from place to place. During the Archaic Period, people became semi-nomadic, traveling less often to areas within their region as the seasons changed. By the Early Woodland Period, this tradition had slowly begun to change once again. The Adena lived in semi-permanent communities. This means

Thomas Worthington's estate, now known as Adena State Park, is located in Chillicothe, Ohio. Worthington was one of Ohio's first U.S. senators and the state's sixth governor. The house was built in 1807 by Benjamin Latrobe, the first architect in the United States.

that they lived in certain areas with groups of families for somewhat longer periods of time. The Adena moved around less than their ancestors had. However, evidence suggests that they did move throughout their immediate areas as the changing seasons affected their food supply.

The Adena were mostly hunters and gatherers of wild plants. However, they also began to plant crops, such as sunflowers, gourds, and squash. Over time, as their traditions involved more planting and harvesting food, the Adena moved less often. They began to build a long-term relationship with their land.

Most scientists believe that the Adena lived in wooden structures made from young trees. These structures were simple shelters covered by branches or animal hides. There is some evidence that has led experts to believe that the Adena built more substantial shelters during the winter. Evidence also suggests that various prehistoric people, including some Adena, used caves as shelters during the harsh winters in the Ohio River Valley.

Adena Mounds

Adena mounds often resembled the natural mounds of earlier times. However, the Adena were the first Native Americans to create artificial mounds of earth in which they buried their dead. While earlier cultural groups had used existing natural glacial kames, the Adena created their mounds. During early archaeological studies, many

Grave Creek Mound, in Moundsville, West Virginia, is one of the largest and most famous Adena burial mounds. Experts believe the mound was built in stages over a period of around 100 years. Grave Creek Mound is 62 feet (18.9 m) high and 240 feet (73.2 m) wide.

Adena mounds were mistaken for Hopewell mounds. Once Adena traits were established, however, many mounds were relabeled as having been built by the Adena.

Most Adena mounds were used for burial purposes. These mounds were generally conical in shape. It is possible that they were modeled after the naturally round mounds made by earlier groups of people. However, Adena burial rituals were more involved than those of their ancestors. Before an actual mound was made, a wooden structure was built that might have served as a tomb. This was a special structure in which the Adena prepared their dead for burial. At times, the Adena placed many bodies in one tomb, like their ancestors had. However, the Adena spent more time arranging the dead in specific positions. It is believed that this arrangement became more complex by the end of the Early Woodland Period.

The Adena had complicated burial ceremonies. Often, they dug pits in the ground in which the remains of a person—most likely one of importance—were buried. Part of constructing the tomb included reinforcing the pit with wood, which made it look like a coffin. Large logs were placed around the burial site.

Archaeologists have actually discovered the burnt remains of these wooden structures in some Adena mounds. At first, they believed that each structure was the home in which the dead person had once lived. Later studies led experts to believe that the structures were

Miamisburg Mound, in Miamisburg, Ohio, is also one of the largest Adena burial mounds. It was originally 68 feet (20.7 m) high and about 300 feet (91.4 m) wide. This painting by artist Charles Sullivan shows an early Ohio settlement near the mound. The painting was done in the mid-nineteenth century.

probably associated with tombs that were built and burned as part of the Adena burial ceremony. Evidence suggests that the remains of Adena people were buried within the structure, and then the structure was burned down. They then began to build the mound over the ashes. As they built the mound, they buried the remains of other Adena at different levels.

Evidence also suggests that the Adena often built new mounds on top of existing ones. In some cases, two small mounds built next to each other were covered and joined by a larger mound. Archaeologists also believe that abandoned Adena mounds were sometimes used again by others later on in prehistoric times.

Other Adena Earthworks

The Adena also built special mounds that were not for burial purposes. These mounds are known as circular earthworks. They have also been referred to as sacred circles or ceremonial circles. They were usually lower and wider than the burial mounds. Some of these earthworks had wooden structures inside. Circular earthworks were similar in shape to the burial mounds, but were surrounded by circular ditches. The ditches were pits from which the soil was taken to build the earthwork.

Adena Artifacts

The Adena buried objects in their mounds along with the remains of their dead. Most of these objects were simple everyday tools made of bone and flint, pipes made of carved pipestone, copper jewelry and headdresses, beads, stone carvings, and clay pots. The development of Adena pottery is an important technological advancement of the Early Woodland Period.

One of the most significant artifacts found in an Adena mound is known as the Adena Pipe. It was found during the excavation of Adena Mound in 1901. The Adena Pipe is different from the plain

The Adena buried tools, such as this arrowhead, in their mounds.

The Adena Pipe was found by archaeologists during an exploration of Adena Mound in 1901.

pipes commonly found in their mounds. This pipe, made of pipe-stone covered in red ocher, was carved into the shape of a human being. The carved details of the clothing and appearance have revealed several aspects of Adena appearance. Experts are unsure of what the pipe represented. The pipe may have represented a person who was a spiritual leader. By looking closely at this unique artifact, archaeologists have come to believe that the pipe represents a man with a goiter, which is a large swelling on the side of the neck caused by disease. The pipe also shows the body of the person to be longer than his legs are. His legs are shorter and thicker than a normal person's legs. Some people believe this may represent a political or religious leader who was a dwarf.

What Happened to the Adena?

We do not know for sure what happened to the Adena people. Early experts believed that they migrated away from the Ohio River Valley as the Hopewell culture developed. Others believed that the Adena were absorbed by the Hopewell culture. Today, it is generally accepted that their culture became more advanced and eventually a different cultural identity was established. We do know that the Adena culture greatly influenced the Hopewell culture. Many Adena lifestyle trends carried on into the Middle Woodland Period for several generations.

Three

The Hopewell

The years from about 100 B.C. to 400 A.D. are known as the Middle Woodland Period. During this time, the Hopewell culture flourished in the southern Ohio Region. Its influence reached across much of the eastern part of the United States. Many groups of people made up the Hopewell culture. The main area of Hopewell occupation was in southern Ohio and in Illinois, near the Mississippi River. This group is known as the Ohio Hopewell Indians. They are also sometimes called the Classical Hopewell. They were named after Captain M. C. Hopewell of Chillicothe, Ohio. More than 30 Hopewell mounds were discovered on his farm.

Many archaeologists believe that the Adena and Hopewell cultures may have existed at the same time in some places. Since no written records exist from this time, it is difficult for experts to define each culture by exact dates. However, two main traits have been identified that separate the Hopewell from all of the Ohio Indians who came before them: their far-reaching system of trade and their complex burial and mound-building traditions.

This painting by artist Louis Glanzman is of a Hopewell burial ceremony.

Hopewell Life

Hopewell Indians were hunters and gatherers, like the Adena. However, the Hopewell relied much more on planting and harvesting crops to fill their basic diet. Squash was one of their most important crops. They also grew a grass called maygrass, an herb called goosefoot, as well as sunflowers, sumpweed, marsh elder, and gourds.

Evidence suggests that the Hopewell society was based on a widespread network of trade. This network is called the Hopewell Interaction Sphere. Bonds between Native American groups in different regions, possibly established earlier by the Adena, grew stronger and reached farther as the Hopewell culture developed. There was an increase in the exchange of ideas and materials from different areas. Archaeologists have found evidence suggesting that the Hopewell Interaction Sphere reached from the Great Lakes to the Gulf of Mexico and from the Atlantic Ocean to the Rocky Mountains. Many Hopewell artifacts were made of materials native to locations far away from Ohio. The Hopewell had shells from Florida, mica from the Appalachian Mountains, shark teeth from the Atlantic Ocean, and obsidian from Wyoming. They also had grizzly bear teeth from the Rocky Mountains and copper from the northern part of Michigan. It is believed that Hopewell communities traded freshwater pearls and chert, a type of rock, in exchange for materials not found naturally in the Ohio area.

The Hopewell Indians created a wealthy and successful society. While there is not enough evidence to prove it, some archaeologists believe that the Hopewell may have influenced a large part of North America culturally and perhaps even politically. It is possible that through travel on the Mississippi River, the Hopewell were able to influence a vast area.

Hopewell Mounds and Earthworks

Hopewell burial mounds were much like Adena mounds in many ways. Their differences, however, show that the Hopewell burial traditions were more complex. These traditions were a very important part of Hopewell society. There are more Hopewell mounds than any other kind. The time in which the Hopewell lived is considered to be the peak of the mound-building era in the Ohio River Valley.

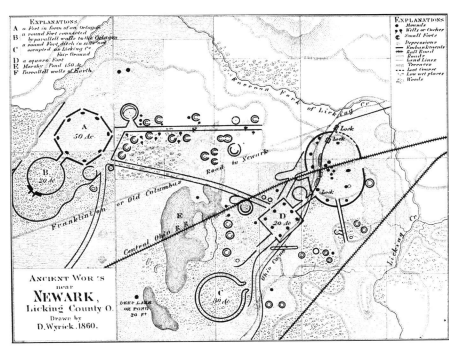

The Newark Earthworks were one of the most complex earthworks built by the Hopewell.

The construction of some Hopewell mounds developed over an extended period of time. Through the work of many generations, the mounds grew larger as the years passed. As their size grew, these mounds and earthworks took on greater importance in the community.

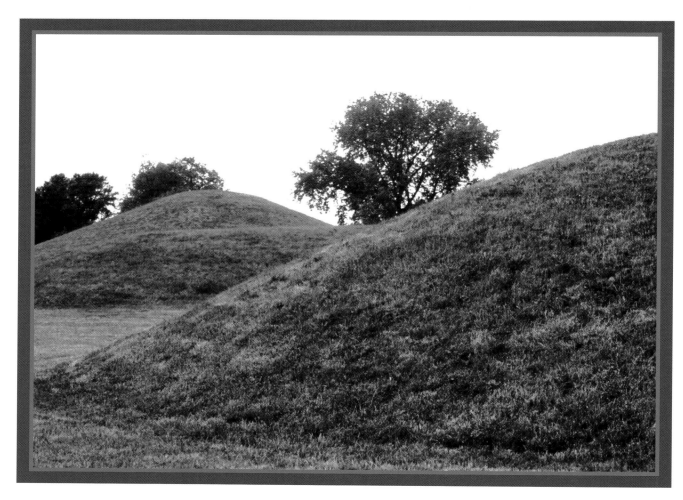

These Hopewell mounds are part of the Hopewell Culture National Historical Park in Chillicothe, Ohio.

It is believed that early in the Middle Woodland Period, groups of related Hopewell families often lived in dwellings near each other. When family members died, they were buried beneath small mounds in the floors of ceremonial structures. Many of the Hopewell were cremated.

No one knows exactly how the Hopewell used these structures. Most experts agree that they were used for burial practices. However, there is also evidence to suggest that some structures may have served ceremonial and social purposes as well.

If a ceremonial structure was no longer considered useful, it was either taken apart or burned. It was then covered with dirt and sometimes with stone and gravel. Experts think that this was a communal ceremony in which all local Hopewell took part. After the ceremony, the Hopewell built a larger mound over all of the smaller mounds they had created.

Ceremonial structures played an important role in Hopewell rituals. Studies of the structures' development over time show how the Hopewell mounds and burial traditions became increasingly complex throughout the Middle Woodland Period. The design of the ceremonial structures varied from a single room to large multi-room complexes. Some people called these larger complexes great rooms. Within these structures, rituals and burials took place. Archaeologists have also discovered bowl-like sections of earth in Hopewell mounds, known as basins, where ritual cremations were performed.

Geometric Earthworks

The Hopewell people built earthworks in addition to their circular mounds. One type of earthwork they created is known as a geometric earthwork. These earthworks are considered the most complex earthworks ever constructed by Hopewellian communities. They were perfectly shaped squares, circles, and other shapes, with parallel walls that stretched on for miles. These earthworks are believed to have been the locations of important Hopewell rituals.

Hilltop Enclosures

Another type of earthwork constructed by the Hopewell is called a hilltop enclosure. Hilltop enclosures are walls of earth located on a hilltop that enclose a specific amount of space. Early scholars believed that hilltop enclosures were actually forts that were used to defend people from attacks by other groups. The tall walls of the enclosures had openings in different places that were thought to have been entrances to the fort. It was believed that these entrances were guarded by wooden gates.

Today, however, it is believed that hilltop enclosures were built for Hopewell ceremonies. Experts think that certain portions of the walls of these enclosures and geometric earthworks were observation points from which the Hopewell watched the movement of the Sun and the moon to keep track of time.

The Marietta Earthworks, in Marietta, Ohio, are examples of geometric earthworks. Many of the mounds were destroyed as the land was developed by settlers.

There is evidence to suggest that the Hopewell used one of their hilltop enclosures as an area of defense. Large logs were found at the Pollack Earthworks in Montgomery County, Ohio. This has led experts to believe that while the site originally served as an area of ceremony, it was also probably used as a place of defense for a short period of time. Experts believe that once the defense area was no longer necessary, the vertical logs were taken down.

Archaeologists have found the remains of Hopewell villages very close to some of these hilltop enclosures. Many people believe that these villages were for a group of people who had gathered from miles away to participate in specific ceremonies at certain times of the year. Evidence suggests that these ceremonial centers were used often. Experts think it is also possible that there was a group of these people who cared for the site for longer periods of time.

Hopewell Artifacts

One of the most visible differences between Adena and Hopewell mounds is the type of artifacts found inside. The Hopewell buried their dead with large numbers of artifacts. Many of these artifacts were more beautifully and expertly made than those of the Adena. In addition to making objects out of local materials, such as flint, Ohio pipestone, and freshwater pearls, the Hopewell also made use of the materials they acquired through trade. In Hopewell burial mounds, archaeologists have uncovered conch shells from the

Archaeologists have found evidence that the Hopewell used a variety of materials to create their works of art. This jewelry, made from freshwater pearls and beaten copper, is believed to have been worn by a Hopewell male.

33

Gulf of Mexico, small amounts of silver from Ontario, obsidian and grizzly bear teeth from the Rocky Mountains, shark teeth from the Atlantic coast, alligator teeth from Louisiana, and mica from North Carolina. Hopewell artifacts include flat shapes and figures cut out of mica, tobacco pipes, and beads made from freshwater pearls and copper. Archaeologists have also found sculptures carved of stone and clay, detailed ornaments, and copper breast-plates. Large quantities of everyday objects, such as tools, hunting equipment, clothing, and pottery, were found as well. On very rare occasions, archaeologists found delicate and decayed pieces of plant fiber that had been made into cloth.

These expertly crafted artifacts made by the Hopewell have helped scientists understand the Hopewell culture. The details of the crafted objects found in Hopewell mounds tell us that the Hopewell were artists who spent time mastering their crafts. Experts believe that they may have even handed down their works of art from one generation to another. The wide variety of materials from many far-off locations shows us that the Hopewell network of trade was highly successful.

We know very little about Hopewell religious customs. Archaeologists have discovered altars in many Hopewell mounds. These altars were surrounded by crafted objects, which have been identified as tools and religious symbols. The altars, the volume of artistic objects found in Hopewell mounds, and their burial practices have led experts to believe that religion was a very

The Hopewell carved flat shapes and figures out of mica. They acquired mica from North Carolina through their widespread network of trade.

36 This clay figure of a Hopewell woman was found at the Turner Mound Group, near Cincinnati, Ohio.

important part of the Hopewell culture. Many Hopewell graves were filled with numerous valuable artifacts and works of Hopewell art. Experts believe that this abundance was a sign of great respect for the person with whom the artifacts were buried.

What Happened to the Hopewell?

For reasons that archaeologists are uncertain of, the Hopewell period came to an end around 400 A.D. This may have been due to a change in the climate, a breakdown in their network of trade, conflict within their society, or problems based on population growth and an increased dependence on crops. Some experts believe that the Hopewell religion may have collapsed. It is possible that Hopewell culture and religion were so intertwined that one may not have been able to exist without the other. Archaeologists have found no evidence of hostility or warfare that would have caused the culture to end. Whatever the cause, the end of the Hopewell culture resulted in several changes in the Ohio Region. It began a period of less interaction between the Native American groups of the Ohio Region. Archaeologists have found evidence of smaller villages and a decrease in artifacts and mounds from this time.

Four

The Fort Ancient

By the end of the Late Woodland Period and into the Late Prehistoric Period, another cultural group developed. Archaeologists call this culture the Fort Ancient people. The Fort Ancient lived in the middle Ohio River Valley from 900 A.D. to the time of European contact around 1650–1700 A.D. The culture stretched from eastern Ohio to southeastern Indiana, and from central Ohio to central Kentucky and western West Virginia. Toward the end of the Late Prehistoric Period, most Fort Ancient communities were located around the Ohio River.

The Fort Ancient Indians were mistakenly named after the Fort Ancient site, a large hilltop enclosure earthwork in southwestern Ohio. Archaeologists found evidence of a large Fort Ancient village at the southern portion of the site. They therefore assumed that the group had also created the hilltop enclosure. However, this was not the case. Later research proved that the Fort Ancient site had actually been created by the Hopewell Indians, more than 1,000 years earlier than experts had originally thought. It became clear that the incorrectly named Fort Ancient Indians had at different times lived in two separate villages on the site, but had not created the large earthwork there.

SunWatch Indian Village, in Dayton, Ohio, is a re-creation of a Fort Ancient village that once existed on that site. Archaeologists reconstructed the village to look the way it did during the time of the Fort Ancient.

Fort Ancient Life

Although hunting and gathering were still a part of their lives, the Fort Ancient Indians were more dependent on agriculture—more than any Native Americans who had come before them. They are recognized as the first true farmers in eastern North America, growing many crops that they and their descendants would come to depend on for survival. They grew large quantities of corn. They also grew beans, squash, sunflowers, and gourds. These crops made up over 75 percent of their diet.

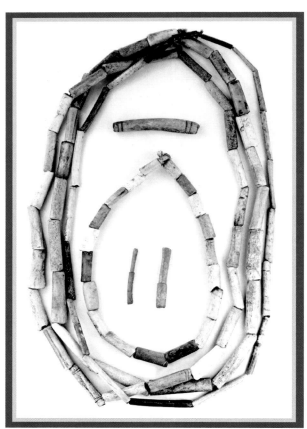

As the production of crops increased, so did the number of people living in villages. Evidence suggests that Fort Ancient people lived in large communities near their farms for much longer periods of time than those that came before them, perhaps as long as 15 to 18 years. They built houses in a circle to enclose a community. In addition, communities were often

This bone bead necklace was found during a 1916 archaeological exploration of a Fort Ancient site in Scioto County, Ohio.

surrounded by a protective fence. Conflict between groups of Native Americans had increased by this time. It was necessary to set up villages defensively for protection.

Fort Ancient Mounds

Very few Fort Ancient mounds have ever been recorded by archaeologists. Unlike the Adena and the Hopewell, the Fort Ancient people were not known for building mounds. Evidence has shown that the Fort Ancient Indians created smaller and far fewer burial mounds than the Hopewell did. When they did use mounds, the Fort Ancient often buried many people in the same mound. The Fort Ancient Indians also created mounds made to resemble figures, especially animals. Artifacts found in Fort Ancient mounds were not as well crafted as those of the Hopewell and were made only from local materials.

What Happened to the Fort Ancient Indians?

The Fort Ancient culture ended when Europeans made contact with the prehistoric peoples of the Ohio area around 1650–1700 A.D. The Europeans who made contact with the prehistoric tribes wrote down information about them, including the names of many tribes.

This marks the end of the Late Prehistoric Period and the beginning of the Historic Period, the time when written records of history were kept. Writings from this time do not discuss the Fort Ancient culture. They describe the native peoples of the area as the Shawnee in southern Ohio, the Miami in the western part of Ohio, the Wyandotte in central Ohio, the Delaware in northeast Ohio, and the Ottawa and the Potawatomi in northwest Ohio.

Serpent Mound

Located in Adams County, Ohio, the Serpent Mound is the largest and most famous Fort Ancient mound in North America. The Serpent Mound is about a quarter of a mile (.4 km) long, four to five feet (1.2 to 1.5 m) tall, and about 20 feet (6.1 m) wide. This mound looks like a long snake with a coiled tail. The snake's mouth looks like it is opening to swallow an oval object, which is thought to be an egg.

The most interesting aspect of this mound is that it is believed to have been used by the Fort Ancient to observe the Sun to record the changing seasons. Experts believe that the Fort Ancient would stand in certain positions and notice the Sun was directly overhead at specific times of year. As they watched the Sun's position change over the course of a year, they knew the seasons were changing. On the right day, the Sun's position over the first curve of the snake, near the tail, marked the first day of winter. The Sun's position over the next curve marked the first day of spring. It is believed that the Sun's position over the third curve marked the first day of summer.

At first, archaeologists thought that the Serpent Mound belonged to the Adena Indians because they found Adena burial mounds nearby. However, further research revealed that the mound is only about 1,000 years old. Although they are still not absolutely certain, most archaeologists have determined that the Serpent Mound is the work of the Fort Ancient Indians. Today, the Serpent Mound is a state memorial that is owned and maintained by the Ohio Historical Society.

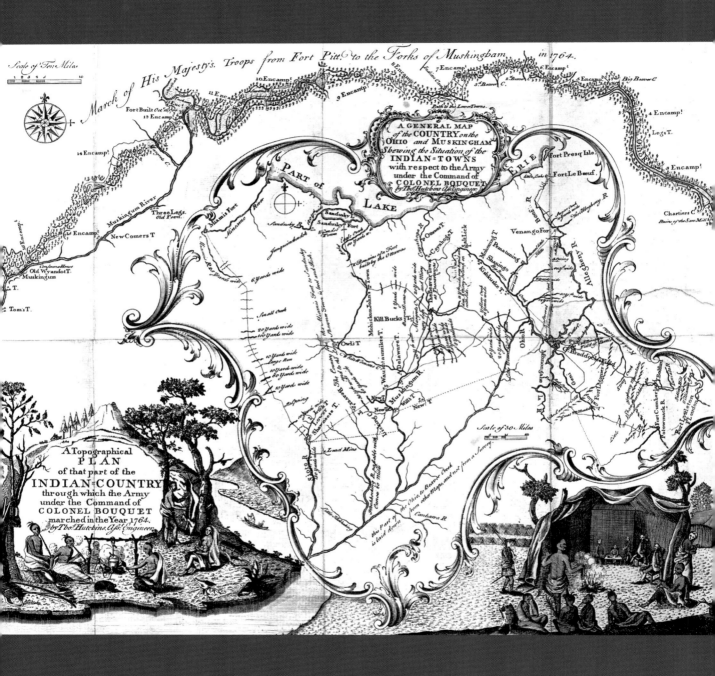

Scale of Ten Miles

+ March of His Majesty's Troops from Fort Pitt, to the Forks of Muskingham, in 1764.

A GENERAL MAP
of the COUNTRY on the
OHIO and MUSKINGHAM
Shewing the Situation of the
INDIAN=TOWNS
with respect to the Army
under the Command of
COLONEL BOUQUET
by Tho.s Hutchins Ass.t Engineer.

PART of LAKE ERIE

Fort Presq Isle
Fort Le Boeuf
Little Lake
Chartiers C.
Ruins of the Saw Mill
Allegheny R.
Venango For.
Kishkushki
Shainingo
Pematuning
Mahoning T.
Kuskuskies T.
Big Beaver C.

Fort Pitt
Ft. Braddocks Field
Monongahela R.
Fort Dequesne
Cumberland R.
Fort Ligonier
Fort London

Sandusky
Sandusky Fort
Wian-dot Town
Junqueindundeh

Miamis Fort
Mineome River

Three Legs
Old Town
New Comers T.

Muskingum River

Conference House
Old Wyandot T.
Muskingum
Tom's T.

Mohickon John's Town
Owl's T.
Waulhaumikee T.
Delaware T.

Kill Bucks T.
Ottawa T.
Salt Lick
Cayahoga R.
Remains of a Fort built by the Ottawas
Big Beaver Town or Tuscarawas

6 Yards wide
Small Creek
20 Yards wide
100 Yards wide
10 Yards wide
60 Yards wide
10 Yards wide
a Spring
Lead Mine

New T.
Muskingum R.
Beaver T.
Tuscarawas T.
Scioto R.

Scale of 50 Miles

this Part of the Ohio to Beaver Creek is laid down from other Maps and not from a Survey.

Canhawa R.

A Topographical
PLAN
of that part of the
INDIAN-COUNTRY
through which the Army
under the Command of
COLONEL BOUQUET
marched in the Year 1764.
by Tho.s Hutchins, Ass.t Engineer.

Five

Mounds During the Historic Period

Europeans began to establish settlements in the Ohio Region during the middle of the eighteenth century. As they moved west, these settlers encountered different mounds in the Ohio Region. Many of these early settlers had little interest in the mounds they encountered in the area. Some Europeans wondered who had built the mounds. Since they considered Native Americans to be primitive, or too uneducated to have constructed such elaborate earthworks, some Europeans believed that the mounds were the work of different cultures from faraway places. Many European settlers simply ignored the mounds altogether.

After the American Revolutionary War ended in 1783, Americans gained their independence from Great Britain. Large groups of Americans moved west, settling the land in and around the Ohio River Valley. As they cleared trees to build communities and farms, many hidden mounds became visible. However, the settlers were much more interested in clearing the land than they were in preserving the mounds. As a result, many mounds were destroyed.

However, there were several groups of people who worked to protect the mounds from being ruined. One group of settlers, called the Ohio Company of Associates, decided to preserve a

This 1764 map of the Ohio River Valley was used by the British army several years before the start of the American Revolutionary War (1775–1783). The British called the area "Indian Country."

mound and earthwork complex they discovered at their Ohio settlement, near the Muskingum River. They set aside the area as a park, which protected the mounds from destruction.

Some influential Americans spoke out in favor of preserving the mounds as records of peoples who no longer existed. Thomas Jefferson, the author of the Declaration of Independence, and Daniel Webster, a respected speaker, spoke to Americans, hoping to convince them that the mounds were an important part of American history. They wanted Americans to feel pride in their new land and its history. While Jefferson and Webster raised some awareness about the importance of the mounds, most Ohio settlers remained uninterested. Over the next few decades, more and more mounds were destroyed to make way for railroad lines, reservoirs, and growing businesses.

Throughout the nineteenth century, people began to gain interest in the mounds of the Ohio River Valley. Still unsure of who had built them, many settlers began to think of the mounds as mysterious representations of a "lost race" of people. This idea is known today as the myth of the mound builders. It was accepted by archaeologists well into the early part of the twentieth century. However, as archaeological methods changed over the years, archaeologists began to look at layers of soil and artifacts more carefully. They realized that the people who built the mounds were not a lost race of people but rather groups of Native Americans who had lived in the area. This led to a shared interest in the mounds as important parts of America's past.

As early Americans began to gain appreciation for the mounds of the Ohio River Valley, some mounds were preserved as parts of national parks. This mound is a part of Hopewell Culture National Historical Park.

As a result of this interest, respected anthropologists and archaeologists began to thoroughly study the mounds. Major investigations of the Ohio mounds and earthworks officially began in the 1820s through the 1840s. Many mounds were explored and turned into national parks.

Many Americans also named places after the mounds. Both Circlesville, Ohio, and Moundsville, West Virginia, were named for the mounds and earthworks located there. Various streets throughout the Ohio Region are named for mounds as well. Businesses, cemeteries, and parks were also named based on the mounds around them.

During the 1900s, archaeologists and anthropologists fought to protect the lands of the ancient mound builders. Although there was a great deal of pressure to develop the land for industrial purposes, several federal acts—such as the Historic Sites and Buildings Act of 1935 and the Archaeological and Historic Preservation Act of 1974—were passed to protect the mounds as historical treasures.

As more mounds and artifacts were discovered and explored, people recognized their importance in understanding the Native Americans who created them. Thanks to careful exploration and study of these mounds, the Adena, Hopewell, and Fort Ancient cultures are remembered today.

Mounds Today

The mounds and earthworks of the Adena, Hopewell, and Fort Ancient Indians are a part of the landscape of the Ohio Region. However, they also help us to uncover the history of the people who built them. Archaeological studies of these creations have provided us with knowledge about these three cultures. The size, location, shape, and type of mound explored have helped experts determine which culture built each one. Artifacts found inside the mounds have also helped experts piece together the history of these prehistoric peoples.

Some of the mounds created by the Adena, Hopewell, and Fort Ancient still exist today. Most of them have been destroyed, while some remain untouched. There were once as many as 10,000 mounds in the Ohio River Valley. Today, however, under 1,000 mounds remain undisturbed. Some mounds have been partially destroyed as land was developed. There are many mounds that can be visited, some as parts of local and national parks. Visiting these mounds and earthworks presents the opportunity to witness history firsthand, bringing the past into the present.

Miamisburg Mound

Miamisburg Mound is one of the largest Adena burial mounds in the eastern United States. Originally, it was 68 feet (20.7 m) high and 877 feet (267.3 m) around at the base. It is located east of the Great Miami River, in Montgomery County, Ohio. Miamisburg Mound was partially explored in 1869, revealing that burials were made at different levels within the mound.

A stone altar was also discovered inside. Different layers of earth, stone, and ash have led archaeologists to believe that Miamisburg Mound was used at different times by the Adena people.

Miamisburg Mound has 117 steps built into its side so that visitors can climb to the top. The mound is under the care of the Miamisburg Parks and Recreation Department and is open all year long.

Hopewell Culture National Historical Park

This site (opposite page) is a complex of Hopewell mounds and earthworks located near Chillicothe, Ohio. The name of this site was Mound City for over 100 years. In 1992, the area was officially renamed the Hopewell Culture National Historical Park. The complex contains the remains of at least 23 mounds and is enclosed within a wooden structure. This is one of the largest known concentrations of Hopewell mounds. Explorations of the many mounds, some of which had been partially or fully destroyed over time, revealed wooden structures within them. Some of the mounds were found to contain many artifacts, such as mica, pipes, copper, and beads.

In 1921, the U.S. Army opened a training camp at Mound City. As a result of this, almost all of the mounds were flattened. However, the grounds of these mounds were preserved. After the training camp was closed, many of the remains of the mounds were explored. Decayed remains of wooden structures and artifacts were found within each one. Some of the mounds, such as Mica Grave Mound, were named based on what was found inside. The largest mound is called Central Mound. It was found to have covered two separate wooden structures, leading experts to believe it was of some importance. The site became a national monument in 1923. The grounds are open for visiting all year long.

Fort Ancient

Fort Ancient is a hilltop enclosure in southwestern Ohio that is three-quarters of a mile (1.2 km) long. Although the name suggests otherwise, Fort Ancient was constructed by the Hopewell Indians. Originally, the site was thought to be the work of the Fort Ancient Indians. However, research done during the early 1940s revealed that the Fort Ancient Indians had in fact used Fort Ancient as a village site 500 years after the Hopewell people had abandoned it as a ceremonial center.

Archaeological evidence has led experts to believe that this Hopewell earthwork was built from 100 B.C. to 260 A.D. and was used for many years after it was built. The Fort Ancient people occupied the site many years later, from around 1000 A.D. to 1200 A.D.

The walls of the earthwork range in height from 3 to 23 feet (.9 m to 7 m) and surround about 125 acres (50.6 ha) of land. Around 18,000 feet (5,486.4 m) of walls made from soil make up the enclosure. There are four mounds within the northeastern portion of the site. From these mounds, people observed the movements of the Sun and the moon to mark the times of the year for certain ceremonies. The Hopewell people had annual rituals and social gatherings involving the Sun. It is believed that they may have used the movement of the moon to mark the decades.

Today, the Fort Ancient site features a museum as well as a garden in which crops are grown to represent the crops grown during the times the Hopewell and Fort Ancient cultures existed. Visiting is allowed during specific hours that can be found by accessing the official Web site through the link on page 62.

Alligator Mound

Alligator Mound (below) is located in Licking County, Ohio. It was built in the shape of what early archaeologists thought was an alligator. Other experts believe that the mound is actually a panther. The mound is close to 250 feet (76.2 m) long and is made of clay, a loose, rocklike material, and stone.

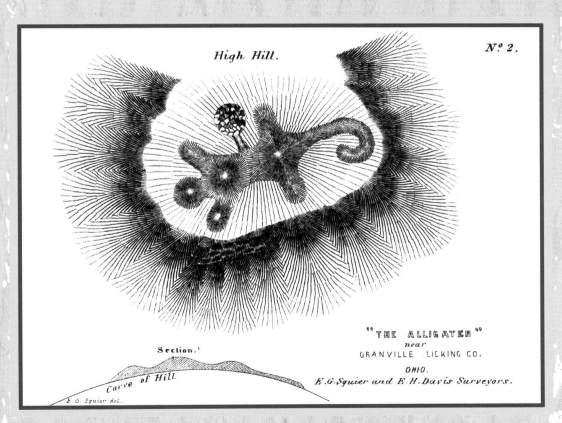

High Hill.

Nº 2.

"THE ALLIGATER"
near
GRANVILLE LICKING CO.

OHIO.

E.G.Squier and E.H.Davis Surveyors.

Section.

Curve of Hill

E.G.Squier del.

Houses have been built on the property surrounding Alligator Mound. However, the mound itself has been preserved by a historical society.

For many years, Alligator Mound was thought to be the work of either the Adena or the Hopewell Indians. In 1999, however, scientific investigations of

the mound proved that it was not as old as experts had originally thought. It is now believed to be the work of the Fort Ancient Indians. Alligator Mound visitors are not allowed to walk on the mound. However, a nearby road provides a clear view of it.

The Adena, Hopewell, and Fort Ancient cultures are an important part of the history of the Ohio River Valley.

Timeline

13,000 to 40,000 years ago	Ancient ancestors of the Native Americans travel from Asia to North America.
13,000 B.C.	Native Americans first come to the area today known as Ohio.
13,000 B.C. to 8000 B.C.	Known as the Paleo-Indian Period, this time represents the earliest well-documented human existence in North America.
8000 B.C. to 1000 B.C.	This period of time is called the Archaic Period. It refers to the years in which the cold and wet weather of the Ice Age ended and a drier, warmer climate emerged.
1000 B.C. to 1650 A.D.–1700 A.D.	Known as the Woodland Period, a time in which the Adena, the Hopewell, and some early Fort Ancient Indians lived in the Ohio Region.

1000 B.C. to 100 B.C.	The Adena Indians live in the Ohio Region.
100 B.C. to 500 A.D.	The Hopewell Indians live in the Ohio Region.
900 A.D. to 1700 A.D.	The Fort Ancient Indians live in the Southern Ohio Region.
1650 A.D. to 1700 A.D.— present	This is called the Historic Period. It refers to the time in which written records exist to document history.
1783	Americans win independence from the British in the American Revolutionary War. Many Americans move west and discover mounds in the Ohio Region. Some mounds are destroyed as land is developed.
1900s	Laws are passed protecting the mounds as archaeological sites. Mounds are explored and recognized as links to the cultures who created them.
Today	Many mounds and earthworks created by the Adena, Hopewell, and Fort Ancient are parts of local and national parks that can be visited.

Glossary

altars (AWL-turz) Large tables in houses of worship used for religious ceremonies.

ancestors (AN-sess-turz) Members of a family who lived a long time ago.

archaeologist (ar-kee-OL-uh-jist) A scientist who studies the past by digging up old buildings and objects and examining them carefully.

artifact (ART-uh-fakt) An object made or changed by human beings, especially a tool or a weapon used in the past.

artificial (ar-ti-FISH-uhl) False, not real, or not natural.

ash (ASH) The powder that remains after something has been burned.

basins (BAY-suhnz) Areas of land carved into the shape of a bowl.

breastplates (BREST-playts) Metal plates worn during ceremonies.

chert (CHIRT) A type of rock used to make stone tools.

coiled (KOILD) Wound around and around into a series of loops.

conch shells (KONCH SHELZ) Spiral shells of different types of marine mollusks.

conical (KAHN-uh-kuhl) Resembling a cone in shape.

cremation (kree-MAY-shun) The burning of a dead body into ashes.

descendants (di-SCEND-uhnts) A family's children, their children, and so on into the future.

disassembled (DISS-uh-sem-buhld) To have taken apart all of the parts of something.

distinct (diss-TINGKT) Clearly different.

dwellings (DWEL-ingz) Places where people live.

earthwork (URTH-work) An embankment or construction made of earth.

evidence (EV-uh-duhnss) Information and facts that help prove something or make you believe that something is true.

excavating (EK-skuh-vay-ting) Digging in the earth, either to put up a building or to search for ancient remains.

flint (FLINT) A gray, hard quartz that produces a spark when struck by steel.

flourished (FLUR-ishd) To have grown and succeeded.

generations (jen-uh-RAY-shuhnz) The descendants from a shared ancestor.

gourds (GORDZ) Plants that were dried and used as containers.

hides (HIDEZ) Animal skins.

kame (KAME) A short ridge, hill, or mound of stratified drift deposited by a melting glacier.

marsh elder (MARSH EL-duhr) A plant that grows in wet, low areas.

memorial (muh-MOR-ee-uhl) Something that is built or done to help people continue to remember a person or an event.

mica (MY-kuh) A mineral that readily separates into very thin sheets.

mound (MOUND) An artificial bank or hill of earth or stones constructed over a burial or ceremonial site.

nomad (NOH-mad) A person who wanders from place to place.

obsidian (uhb-SIH-dee-uhn) A dark natural glass formed by the cooling of molten lava.

ocher (OH-kurh) An iron ore used as a pigment.

perishable (PER-ish-uh-buhl) Likely to spoil or decay quickly.

pipestone (PIPE-stohn) A pink or mottled pink-and-white stone used especially by American Indians to make carved objects.

primitive (PRIM-uh-tiv) Basic and crude.

reservoirs (REZ-ur-vwarz) Natural or artificial holding areas for large amounts of water.

substantial (suhb-STAN-shuhl) Solidly built; strong or firm.

sumpweed (SUMP-weed) A green plant that has seeds and grows in Midwestern wetlands.

Resources

BOOKS

Brose, David S., and N'Omi Greber. *Hopewell Archaeology: The Chillicothe Conference.* Kent, OH: Kent State University Press, 1979.

Caldwell, Joseph R., and Robert L. Hall (eds.). *Hopewellian Studies.* Springfield, IL: Illinois State Museum, 1977.

Dragoo, Don W. *Mounds for the Dead.* Pittsburgh, PA: Carnegie Museum of Natural History, 1989.

Silverberg, Robert. *The Mound Builders.* Athens, OH: Ohio University Press, 1986.

Woodward, Susan L., and Jerry N. McDonald. *Indian Mounds of the Middle Ohio Valley: A Guide to Mounds and Earthworks of the Adena, Hopewell, Cole, and Fort Ancient People.* Blacksburg, VA: McDonald & Woodward Publishing Company, 2002.

WEB SITES

Due to the changing nature of Internet links, PowerKids Press has developed an online list of Web sites related to the subject of this book. This site is updated regularly. Please use this link to access the site:

http://www.powerkidslinks.com/lna/ohio

Index